AT THE WELL

*Discovering God's Plan
for Finding True Love*

KRISTEN TIBER

ISBN 978-0-9995876-0-7

www.KristenTiber.com

Dedication

TO DAN, YOU ARE THE love of my life and I am ever thankful to the Lord that I am able to call you mine.

To Lydia, our Eliezer. I am sorry we could not accommodate your request of naming our firstborn after you. But a boy named Lydia invites way too much trouble. I hope this suffices.

To my kids, who bring such joy and fullness to our lives. You are a blessing!

To the many young adults we know who are in the perfect place to meet the one God has for you. Be patient. Be fearless. Live at the well.

To Jesus, the best matchmaker of all time and great lover of our souls. I am forever grateful.

TABLE OF CONTENTS

Part Four: Meeting at the Well

Part Five: Living at the Well

INTRODUCTION

I F YOU WERE TO SIT down at a coffee shop with a group of married couples and ask how they met, you would hear a variety of stories. Some would say they met their spouse at college. Others would tell you they were high school sweethearts and have been together as long as they can remember. There will be those who share how they met at work and some who say they met at the gym. I would tell you that I met my husband on a blind date. That is the fact of our meeting.

However, the truth behind the story is that I met Dan *at the well*.

But wait, I'm getting ahead of myself . . .

It is rare to meet a single person who doesn't hope someday to be married. Most people think of life down the road and see themselves with another person. I did. They hope for that happy life as husband and wife, later to be followed by little ones. And I imagine if you are reading this book, you too desire to spend your life with someone wonderful.

But in all the hopes we have for our future, there is something dangerous about the way we approach dating and marriage as a culture. One look at our divorce rates reveals a profound problem. Maybe you have known people who rush into new or escalating relationships. You may have friends who are so desperate to date and be with someone for the social status or simply because they dislike being alone. Maybe your friend married someone who *everyone else* knew wasn't right for him or her and now you see their struggling relationship.

When I was a wedding planner, I had the opportunity to work with many engaged couples. I saw firsthand how couples would handle various forms of conflict . . . from little disagreements over trivial items to the big financial decisions. I saw couples who were well matched and handled each challenge with ease. Not that there was never conflict, it was simply they were mature enough to handle it well and for each other's benefit. These were the couples who could work together and balance each other.

But unfortunately, I also saw a handful of couples who were so focused on the wedding, they forgot to plan for a successful marriage. The stress of wedding planning revealed a rush to the altar, their lack of compatibility, their inability to handle conflict as a couple and their omission to really consider whether they were well-suited for each other.

I suspect that is not the kind of relationship you want. Maybe you have realized that you want something different, something better. A good match. The right person. A divinely arranged marriage. A relationship that God Himself orchestrates through the wonder of His love, the beauty of His kindness, and His intense knowledge of and affection for you!

In this book, we will talk about God's plan for romance. And although sometimes the journey is challenging, we will see why it is important to seek God in the pursuit of relationships. We will work through what you can be doing right now to prepare yourself, where you can meet that man or woman, how to evaluate a relationship for marriage and ultimately, the incredible blessings of doing this God's way.

Who am I? I am just an ordinary person with an incredible testimony, someone who yielded and allowed God to be in control and write a love story straight from heaven. And this can be yours too. God is interested in your love story. When you decide to follow the journey we talk about in this book, you will be amazed at the detail, at the design, at the grand plan and overflowing joy that can be your own testimony. I can think of countless others who have followed God's plan in their own relationships and found true love.

Don't wait to start this journey. Save yourself the heartache and scars that come from bad relationships and poor decisions. Don't settle for an unhappy marriage. Rather look for that love that is God-designed. Are you ready to pursue it?

Let's look at God's plan for true love.

It's time to head to the well.

Part One
Going to the Well

Pack Your Bag

Chapter One

WELCOME! TODAY, WE START AN exciting journey together. How often my husband and I have sat down with young adults and talked about love, romance and marriage. And how I wish we could meet for coffee (or the diet soda that I probably drink too much) and talk about where you are on this journey toward love and the altar.

Perhaps you are in a relationship right now. Maybe you are coming out of a relationship or you are watching all your friends pair off like the couples on Noah's ark and you're feeling like a bit of an outsider to life's typical path.

Wherever you are, the path in this book is anything but typical. It isn't something the masses are doing. It isn't the popular way of finding love. But it is real. And it is wonderful. I can tell you, even from my own experience, that this journey will be one of the best adventures of your life.

Pack a bag because throughout the pages of this book, we will be setting up camp and getting pretty comfortable with Genesis 24. It is a precious story and beautiful illustration of God's design and arrangement for the marriage of a man and woman.

Their names? Isaac and Rebekah.

But before we begin, let me set the stage for you.

Isaac was the son God promised to Abraham. Abraham and his wife, Sarah, being quite along in years, had never had children and didn't expect to at their age. But God had made a covenant with Abraham. Among the promises of the covenant were that Abraham would be the father of many nations (Genesis 17:4) and that his descendants would be numerous like the stars of the sky (Genesis 22:17).

To a barren couple of old age, this must have sounded impossible. Both Abraham and Sarah laughed at the prospect of parenthood. But as you may know, with God anything is possible (Matthew 19:26). The Lord told them to name their son Isaac . . . which actually means laughter. Don't you love God's own sense of humor?

You may have heard people using the names of Abraham, Isaac and Jacob together in sequence. This is because these three men are the patriarchs of the Jewish and Christian faiths. In the Bible, you'll hear about the God of Abraham, Isaac and Jacob. While these three were not perfect men, they were the ones that God used to establish His covenant and whisper the coming of His son, Jesus.

As we approach Genesis 24, Sarah has died and Abraham grows concerned for the future of his son, Isaac. Abraham had other children through other wives, but Isaac was the one who was the child of promise. It would be through his lineage that God would bless all other nations.

Let's read through our story. We're going to read it all in one sitting, but we'll be breaking it down into sections as we go along.

Genesis 24

> Abraham was now very old, and the Lord had blessed him in every way. He said to the senior servant in his household, the one in charge of all that he had, "Put your hand under my thigh. I want you to swear by the Lord, the God of heaven and the God of earth, that you will not get a wife for my son from the daughters of the Canaanites, among whom I am living, but will go to my country and my own relatives and get a wife for my son Isaac."

The servant asked him, "What if the woman is unwilling to come back with me to this land? Shall I then take your son back to the country you came from?"

"Make sure that you do not take my son back there," Abraham said. "The Lord, the God of heaven, who brought me out of my father's household and my native land and who spoke to me and promised me on oath, saying, 'To your offspring I will give this land'—he will send his angel before you so that you can get a wife for my son from there. If the woman is unwilling to come back with you, then you will be released from this oath of mine. Only do not take my son back there." So the servant put his hand under the thigh of his master Abraham and swore an oath to him concerning this matter.

Then the servant left, taking with him ten of his master's camels loaded with all kinds of good things from his master. He set out for Aram Naharaim and made his way to the town of Nahor. He had the camels kneel down near the well outside the town; it was toward evening, the time the women go out to draw water.

Then he prayed, "Lord, God of my master Abraham, make me successful today, and show kindness to my master Abraham. See, I am standing beside this spring, and the daughters of the townspeople are coming out to draw water. May it be that when I say to a young woman, 'Please let down your jar that I may have a drink,' and she says, 'Drink, and I'll water your camels too'—let her be the one you have chosen for your servant Isaac. By this I will know that you have shown kindness to my master."

Before he had finished praying, Rebekah came out with her jar on her shoulder. She was the daughter of Bethuel son of Milkah, who was the wife of Abraham's brother Nahor. The woman was very beautiful, a virgin; no man had ever slept with her. She went down to the spring, filled her jar and came up again.

The servant hurried to meet her and said, "Please give me a little water from your jar."

"Drink, my lord," she said, and quickly lowered the jar to her hands and gave him a drink.

After she had given him a drink, she said, "I'll draw water for your camels too, until they have had enough to drink." So she quickly emptied her jar into the trough, ran back to the well to draw more water, and drew enough for all his camels. Without saying a word, the man watched her closely to learn whether or not the Lord had made his journey successful.

When the camels had finished drinking, the man took out a gold nose ring weighing a beka and two gold bracelets weighing ten shekels. Then he asked, "Whose daughter are you? Please tell me, is there room in your father's house for us to spend the night?"

She answered him, "I am the daughter of Bethuel, the son that Milkah bore to Nahor." And she added, "We have plenty of straw and fodder, as well as room for you to spend the night."

Then the man bowed down and worshiped the Lord, saying, "Praise be to the Lord, the God of my master Abraham, who has not abandoned his kindness and faithfulness to my master. As for me, the Lord has led me on the journey to the house of my master's relatives."

The young woman ran and told her mother's household about these things. Now Rebekah had a brother named Laban, and he hurried out to the man at the spring. As soon as he had seen the nose ring, and the bracelets on his sister's arms, and had heard Rebekah tell what the man said to her, he went out to the man and found him standing by the camels near the spring. "Come, you who are blessed by the Lord," he said. "Why are you standing out here? I have prepared the house and a place for the camels."

So the man went to the house, and the camels were unloaded. Straw and fodder were brought for the camels, and water for him and his men to wash their feet. Then food was set before him, but he said, "I will not eat until I have told you what I have to say."

"Then tell us," Laban said.

So he said, "I am Abraham's servant. The Lord has blessed my master abundantly, and he has become wealthy. He has given him sheep and cattle, silver and gold, male and female servants, and camels and donkeys. My master's wife Sarah has borne him a son in her old age,and he has given him everything he owns. And my master made me swear an oath, and said, 'You must not get a wife for my son from the daughters of the Canaanites, in whose land I live, but go to my father's family and to my own clan, and get a wife for my son.'

"Then I asked my master, 'What if the woman will not come back with me?'

"He replied, 'The Lord, before whom I have walked faithfully, will send his angel with you and make your journey a success, so that you can get a wife for my son from my own clan and from my father's family. You will be released from my oath if, when you go to my clan, they refuse to give her to you—then you will be released from my oath.'

"When I came to the spring today, I said, 'Lord, God of my master Abraham, if you will, please grant success to the journey on which I have come. See, I am standing beside this spring. If a young woman comes out to draw water and I say to her, "Please let me drink a little water from your jar," and if she says to me, "Drink, and I'll draw water for your camels too," let her be the one the Lord has chosen for my master's son.'

"Before I finished praying in my heart, Rebekah came out, with her jar on her shoulder. She went down to the spring and drew water, and I said to her, 'Please give me a drink.'

"She quickly lowered her jar from her shoulder and said, 'Drink, and I'll water your camels too.' So I drank, and she watered the camels also.

"I asked her, 'Whose daughter are you?'

"She said, 'The daughter of Bethuel son of Nahor, whom Milkah bore to him.'

"Then I put the ring in her nose and the bracelets on her arms, and I bowed down and worshiped the Lord. I praised the Lord, the God of my master Abraham, who had led me on the right road to get the granddaughter of my master's brother for his son. Now if you will show kindness and faithfulness to my master, tell me; and if not, tell me, so I may know which way to turn."

Laban and Bethuel answered, "This is from the Lord; we can say nothing to you one way or the other. Here is Rebekah; take her and go, and let her become the wife of your master's son, as the Lord has directed."

When Abraham's servant heard what they said, he bowed down to the ground before the Lord. Then the servant brought out gold and silver jewelry and articles of clothing and gave them to Rebekah; he also gave costly gifts to her brother and to her mother. Then he and the men who were with him ate and drank and spent the night there.

When they got up the next morning, he said, "Send me on my way to my master."

But her brother and her mother replied, "Let the young woman remain with us ten days or so; then you may go."

But he said to them, "Do not detain me, now that the Lord has granted success to my journey. Send me on my way so I may go to my master."

Then they said, "Let's call the young woman and ask her about it." So they called Rebekah and asked her, "Will you go with this man?"

"I will go," she said.

So they sent their sister Rebekah on her way, along with her nurse and Abraham's servant and his men. And they blessed Rebekah and said to her,

"Our sister, may you increase
to thousands upon thousands;
may your offspring possess
the cities of their enemies."

Then Rebekah and her attendants got ready and mounted the camels and went back with the man. So the servant took Rebekah and left.

Now Isaac had come from Beer Lahai Roi, for he was living in the Negev. He went out to the field one evening to meditate, and as he looked up, he saw camels approaching. Rebekah also looked up and saw Isaac. She got down from her camel and asked the servant, "Who is that man in the field coming to meet us?"

"He is my master," the servant answered. So she took her veil and covered herself.

Then the servant told Isaac all he had done. Isaac brought her into the tent of his mother Sarah, and he married Rebekah. So she became his wife, and he loved her; and Isaac was comforted after his mother's death.

There are so many treasures in this story that are calling out to me for attention. What did you pick up on? What I see over everything else is that God is interested in whom Isaac marries. And my friend, He is just as interested in who you marry.

If by the end of this book, I haven't completely convinced you that God has a plan for you, I have failed. Throughout these pages, we will walk this road together . . . figuring out God's plan for true love and what is His best for your life. Are you ready to dig in and discover the gold nuggets of God's plan in this love story? I hope so!

Let's start by taking a look at Abraham and his servant. In our narrative, we never learn the identity of the servant. He does not use his own name, but only refers to himself as Abraham's servant. Many scholars believe him to be Eliezer, the chief servant of Abraham. He had been with Abraham a long time and would have been Abraham's heir had a son not been born.[1]

This servant in our story (who we will assume is Eliezer) must have loved Abraham very much to take on such an important quest. He sets off with 10 camels loaded with "all kinds of good things" and the blessing and instructions of his master.

Now, the journey would have been long. Some believe it would have taken weeks, perhaps more than a month.[2] Upon reaching his destination, where does this old, faithful servant go? Does he knock on doors? Does he go to the rich or to the most popular socialites of the day? No.

He goes to the well outside the town . . . right about the time the women would be coming out to draw water. (The words *well* and *spring* are used interchangeably in the story to describe the same place.)

Let's pause for just a moment right here.

You see, several times in Scripture, the well is used as an illustration for God. In Psalm 36:9, David says, "For with you is the fountain of life . . . ." Isaiah 12:3 states, "With joy you will draw water from the wells of salvation." Our salvation is from the Lord. He is the source. He is the well. Not only is Genesis 24 a true story, but it is also a beautiful image for the faith-filled life.

In John 4, we see another well. Jesus meets the Samaritan woman at the well and asks her for a drink. She questions His request because He is a Jew, she is a Samaritan and Jews did not associate with Samaritans. However, the gold is in His reply. "If you knew the gift of God and who it is that asks you for a drink, you would have asked him and he would have given you living water" (John 4:10). Jesus is the source of living water. What is this living water? It is our salvation, paid for by His own blood while we were still sinners. It is the Spirit of God living within us guaranteeing our inheritance as His children. It is a life lived anew, putting away the past and walking forward living for Him. It is transforming, redeeming and overflowing.

Why is this so important? Because, before we can pursue a relationship toward a godly marriage with another human being, we need to first visit the well for ourselves. We need to be right with the Creator of the universe. We need to be in a relationship with Him.

Before you meet your future spouse, you need to meet and know the One who created both of you. He is the One who wrote the greatest love story of all time.

Have you heard it? Do you know the Gospel story? Do you know the freedom, love, grace and mercy that can be yours in Jesus? There is a holy, just and loving God who created the heavens and the earth . . . who created you. But sin, the things we do wrong, the thoughts and acts of disobedience to what He has commanded, keeps us from knowing and loving Him. Sin is like a wall that separates us from Him.

But the Bible tells us that He loved us so much that He sent His one and only Son to pay the price for our sin (this is called redemption) so that the wall can be broken down and we may have a relationship with Him. The punishment for sin that should have been ours, was paid by God's Son. Because of what Jesus did on the cross, we can stand in His righteousness (and not in our sinful rags) before this holy and loving God.

Through Jesus' death and resurrection not only comes the promise of life eternal in His presence but also a relationship with Him. You see God, the Father, has always wanted a relationship with His children. He loves us. He loves us so much that He sent Jesus to face all kinds of horribleness just to allow us to be close to Him, as originally created.

Some think doing good deeds can earn them their way to heaven. But what is the measure for good enough? No, salvation is completely and wholly a gift. Based nothing on what we have done or could do. The Scriptures say, "For it is by grace you have been saved, through faith—and this not from yourselves, it is the gift of God—not by works, so that no one can boast" (Ephesians 2:8-9).

Salvation is solely by grace through faith. Romans 10:9 tells us, "That if you confess with your mouth, 'Jesus is Lord,' and believe in your heart that God raised him from the dead, you will be saved." What are you saved from? You are saved from the punishment of your sin and an eternity without Him.

I was saved as a child. I was probably about age six or seven when I understood what Jesus did for me, believing He died on the cross for my sin and rose from the dead, conquering death. I had a tender heart for Him and I am thankful I was so young.

My husband, Dan, didn't come to the Lord until he was 26 years old. And you know what? Even though we were raised one small town away from each other, the Lord didn't have us meet until after he was a believer. (Incidentally, you don't know where your future spouse may be in his or her faith. It's a great reason to pray for this person!)

My friend, if you hope to have a godly and fulfilling love story, you need to understand the length to which the Lord went to secure your relationship with Him. You need to seek Him first before seeking love.

Like Eliezer, go to the well. Find that spot of life-giving water, that sweet place where you are seeking after Him.

But it doesn't stop there. Let's see what happens next in Chapter Two.

Part Two
Growing at the Well

Draw Your Water

Chapter Two

I DON'T KNOW IF I could have lived in pioneer days. I am all too accustomed to flushing toilets, water on demand at my kitchen sink and, you know, that wonderful thing called electricity. Some days, however, I think I could do without all the technology at my fingertips. The slower life does look appealing in that respect. But please, don't leave me without running water, my washing machine or my dishwasher.

Rebekah knew of no such conveniences. Not only did she not have the luxury of a kitchen sink, but she also had to trek to the well every day. Think about how much water you use in the course of one day. Now imagine you have to carry all that water from a well back to your home. All I can say is "Go Rebekah!" and be quite thankful that we live in a different time.

> He had the camels kneel down near the well outside
> the town; it was toward evening, the time the women
> go out to draw water. (Genesis 24:11)

Women in the east would have gone out twice a day to draw water for their families, in the morning and in the evening.[3] The second trip would have happened at the cool of the day when the heat was subsiding and the evening breeze was beginning to stir.[4] The women would have completed a full day of work and once again returned to the well to get water to sustain themselves and their families until the next day.

The women made regular trips to the well. What can we take away from this? If the well represents that place, that quiet spot where we meet with the Lord, then our story is reminding us that we need to meet with God regularly. As real as our need for water in daily living, so is the need to draw spiritual water through time spent with God.

This morning during our devotional time, I talked with my kids about being in a relationship with God. It is one thing to believe. It is one thing to know *about* Him. But it is another thing to know Him personally.

We have a relational God who desires to have a relationship with you! Yes, the Creator of the universe wants to be close to you. He formed you in your mother's womb (Psalm 139:13). He oversees all your comings and goings (Psalm 121:8). He sets His angels to guard you

(Psalm 91:11). You are the apple of His eye (Psalm 17:8) and He has good plans for you (Jeremiah 29:11).

One of my favorite verses in the Bible is Philippians 3:10. It is written by the apostle Paul and says, "I want to know Christ . . . ." You may hear this and think "C'mon, Paul. You know Christ. Jesus appeared to you on the road to Damascus. You have preached about Him, you've taught about Him. Not only are you the apostle to the Gentiles, but you are also the author of many New Testament epistles. What do you mean you want to know Christ? You already do!"

But a closer look at the Greek for the word "know" will reveal something much more than a knowledge of something or someone. Paul uses the Greek word that means to know intimately, to understand,5 . . . to know relationally. Paul, the great apostle Paul, is telling us that there is so much more than simply the knowledge of God. Paul is hungry to know Him better, to be closer to this risen Christ. Do you hunger like that? Pause for a moment and ask Him to stir a hunger and thirst for Him.

Just as Rebekah went daily to the well for water, we too need to go to the well to meet with God regularly. It is the place where we are not only seeking Him as in Chapter One, but the place where we are also growing in faith and our relationship with Him, and He is growing us as an individual.

Let's look at two areas of necessary growth that you can be working on before you meet the person you will marry.

Growing in Faith and Relationship with the Lord

I am terrible with indoor plants . . . well, many outdoor plants too. Okay, maybe I should say anything in a pot is in danger around me. When I first plant my spring annuals in the two large pots on my front porch, I do a great job remembering to water them every day. I fill my pitcher and happily nourish my plants. My thumb actually looks a little green!

But then a few weeks in, I miss a day of watering. And once this day comes, I know it is all downhill. One day turns into three (and four and five) and before I know it, the flowers are looking ratty . . . and brown . . . then dead. But they still sit on my front porch (probably to the dismay of my neighbors). I failed. I didn't nurture my plants on a regular basis. They didn't grow because I didn't do what they needed to continue growing.

As we have said, a strong relationship with the Lord takes regular seeking . . . regular visits to that well where we find life-giving water. This isn't about relationships with other people. This is about you and Him. It is about pursuing Him and finding that He has been chasing after you all this time.

How do we grow closer to the Lord? Through study of His Word, through prayer and the fellowship of other believers. If you are not in a Bible-teaching church, find one and get involved. Attend church regularly. Join a Bible study group or start one if it doesn't already exist.

You will see your faith grow and know Him more intimately as you prioritize your relationship with God. You will need to choose Him over other things. As you do this and as you grow closer to the Lord, you will notice that your desires begin to align more with His. You want what He wants. You discover the truth that His plan is far better than what you may have chosen previously.

And my friend, this is key as you pursue love. There will be times when you so badly want to be dating someone or wish you could change the status on your social media to "In Relationship." However, as you grow in your relationship with the Lord, you will find an increasing trust that He will bring the right person at the right time. You'll be okay staying single a bit longer because you're not interested in dating someone who clearly isn't a match for you. You know He has something better in store.

The other part of growing in our relationship with God is obedience. This is not an easy concept for our culture. The idea of submitting to anyone or anything is foreign in our "I control my own destiny" ingrained world. But obedience is crucial for the Christian walk. God clearly sets out right from wrong in the Bible. We need to obey in the little things as well as the big.

When we seek to grow our relationship with the Lord, you will notice that God pours out His blessings over every area of your life. This doesn't mean everything is perfect. You simply see with fresh eyes the blessings He has given you. Read what Beth Moore, a popular Bible teacher, says in her study, *The Patriarchs*: "Without exception, every area of my life has been affected positively by a growing intimacy with God. When we seek to be fully His, blessing overflows the walls of our compartmentalized lives."[6]

Growing as an Individual

As we visit the well each day, be sure to stay tuned-in on how God wants you to grow as a person. What garden in your life needs to be watered and what weeds need to be pulled?

When looking for a spouse, you need to *be* the type of person that would be attractive to the kind of person you want. Do you want someone who has a kind spirit? Then, strive to be kind. Do you want someone who seeks after God with his or her whole heart? Then, you too need to do this. Do you want someone who prioritizes family? Then be sure that you are making your family a priority.

Let me phrase it another way. If you want someone who is honest and trustworthy and you find that man or woman, do you think a trustworthy individual is going to desire that in a spouse as well? Absolutely. Be the kind of person that he or she is looking to meet and marry.

Another aspect of growing as an individual is to take a look at your other relationships. Are there areas on which you need to work? Do you need to be better at communication? Do you need to improve on voicing your concerns or speaking up for yourself? Are you passive or aggressive in your communication style? Do you need to be more assertive? Maybe you need to be more understanding, empathetic or learn how to reign in a quick temper. These are all things you can be working on now. Pick up a book at the library or search the internet for help improving one of these areas.

Think about the relationship examples you have had in your life. What does a godly relationship and marriage look like? If you haven't had a good example of marriage from your own family, look to other couples in your church who have strong marriages. Take notice of how they treat and talk to one another.

Think about issues in your previous dating relationships. What worked? What didn't work? Is there an area in which you need to mature? Should you have handled things differently in that past relationship? Learn from your mistakes.

This is the time to prayerfully take inventory of how God wants you to grow. Find someone you respect and look up to in the faith (of the same gender) and ask him or her to have a cup of coffee. Ask questions. Request prayer. Maybe you'll find a mentoring relationship that God will use to bless you.

Whether talking with a trusted friend or family member, reading a book on communication or searching the internet for specific tips that will help you overcome a challenge, this is prime time for allowing God to stretch and grow you as a person.

As we wrap up growing at the well in our faith and as an individual, I want to share with you one of the best illustrations I have heard for meeting your mate. Tommy Nelson shares it in his study of the Song of Solomon.

Picture yourself running a race. This is the race you are running as you follow God. You run hard and you run fast, keeping your eyes straight ahead on Jesus, pursuing your relationship with Him.

After you've been running for a while, look to each side and take notice of who is running near you. Then, run more! Later, once again, look to your side and see who is keeping up. Say hi and then, run some more. And if they are still keeping up with you farther in the race, then you can join each other . . . and run together.[7]

The most awesome kind of marriage is when two individuals who love and follow Jesus decide to do life together, following after God . . . together. But you won't meet that follower of Jesus unless you are running the race as well.

Grow in your faith. Grow as a person in the ways God leads you. Be praying for your future spouse. And as we'll see next, sometimes God moves in response to our prayer quickly and other times, it requires a little something called patience.

Part Three

Waiting at the Well

Trust Means What?

Chapter Three

I ATTENDED A CHRISTIAN SCHOOL in western Pennsylvania, Grove City College. It was a wonderful four years of my life where my faith was strengthened, I was stretched and challenged, and I had the pleasure of meeting other believers, several of whom became lifelong friends.

I can remember on the first day of freshman orientation, the Vice President of Student Affairs came out in her bright red dress and said the following phrase to all of the freshman class. She said,

> Look to your left. Look to your right.
> Your future mate may be in sight.

Now I understand the beauty of being at a Christian school with so many like-minded men and women. It *could* be the perfect place to meet one's future spouse.

Same faith, same passion, same world-view. It does sound glorious for pursuing the dating scene, doesn't it?

However, this mindset of "ooh, my future husband or wife could be sitting right next to me . . . or be in my humanities class . . . or be in my study group . . . or, or, or," didn't always help the focus stay on God for providing a future mate.

This kind of thinking without the balanced approach of waiting on God could and did work an urgency in the hearts of some students who were in a hurry to find a mate while at college because *that is what you're supposed to do*. Have you ever felt pressured to find your mate and settle down?

Now, I will tell you that I had many friends who met their spouse at the college and have wonderful marriages. What a blessing to meet your husband or wife in such an environment and have the many opportunities to grow in faith together that are often present at a Christian school.

However, this wasn't my story. Nor was it the story of my roommate and two suitemates. All of us met our husbands off the college campus and out in the real world. (Although one of our husbands did attend the same college at the same time . . . it just comes down to God's timing.)

When we are in search of a future spouse, it always means trusting God. And sometimes trusting means waiting.

Let's look at Genesis 24. Abraham has asked his servant to go to his country and find a wife for Isaac. For context, we'll start back in verse 10 when the servant is leaving on his mission.

> Then the servant left, taking with him ten of his master's camels loaded with all kinds of good things from his master. He set out for Aram Naharaim and made his way to the town of Nahor. He had the camels kneel down near the well outside the town; it was toward evening, the time the women go out to draw water.
>
> Then he prayed, "Lord, God of my master Abraham, make me successful today, and show kindness to my master Abraham. See, I am standing beside this spring, and the daughters of the townspeople are coming out to draw water. May it be that when I say to a young woman, 'Please let down your jar that I may have a drink,' and she says, 'Drink, and I'll water your camels too'—let her be the one you have chosen for your servant Isaac. By this I will know that you have shown kindness to my master." (Genesis 24:10-14)

Notice in our story in Genesis 24 that Abraham's servant didn't rush off in search of a wife for Isaac. He got to the well and he prayed. He intended to wait on God, not to take matters into his own hands. He prayed and sat under the leadership of God.

We need to know and realize that waiting is okay! In our culture, we wait for nothing. Want to know the weather? Tap the app on your phone for an instant weather update. Curious about how your favorite sports team played? No need to wait for the evening news, just open your sports app and check. Don't want to simply wait at the doctor's office? Stay occupied by sending a couple of text messages, deleting emails or playing a game.

We no longer know how to wait. I know it is super convenient with all this technology at our fingertips. In fact just this morning, I asked Siri to tell me the differences between hurricane categories. I didn't have to wait at all. Up popped a link with a full description on categories one through five. Amazing, right?

But in all this instant gratification and lack of waiting, have our hearts followed our culture's pattern when it comes to the things of God? Are we quick to rush and fast to move? Have we forgotten that waiting on the Lord brings a set of blessings all its own?

As I mentioned earlier, I was a child when I was saved. I was blessed to grow up knowing and growing in a relationship with the Lord. I could have met my husband at any point in high school or college and been able to pursue a godly relationship toward marriage with a like-minded individual. I dated a nice, Christian guy at the end of high school and into college, but after that I didn't really date much. When that relationship ended or when I finished college, why didn't God bring me the man I was going to marry right away? Why didn't it happen quickly?

Simply put, it wasn't God's time. Dan was not ready. He wasn't yet saved. He had grown up in church and was raised in the faith, but he didn't know Jesus as Lord and Savior until he was 26 years old. You see, God knew what He was doing. I wouldn't have even considered pursuing a relationship with someone who didn't share the same core beliefs and passion for God that I had. The Lord needed to prepare and grow me for Dan but He also had to prepare Dan for me.

It is easy to think that God has forgotten you when it comes to matching you up with someone. But I can tell you with full confidence, He has not forgotten you. He sees you. (I have something so beautiful to share with you on this point, but it will have to wait for later in our story. Stay tuned!)

The One whom you have trusted with your salvation and eternity can certainly be trusted with the details of your love life. In all those years, I never doubted that God had someone for me. And if He planned that for *me*, I know He has that planned for you.

Waiting at the well takes faith to believe, purpose to persevere and patience to wait. It takes courage to be alone for this set duration of time . . . to say no to a relationship when you know it is clearly opposed to God's plan for your life. Waiting doesn't mean a passive position. Waiting on God is an active choice you make.

Waiting means trusting God to lead you.

"May the God of hope fill you with all joy and peace as you trust in him, so that you may overflow with hope by the power of the Holy Spirit." Romans 15:13

What to Do in the Meantime

- Continue to grow as we spoke about in the last chapter.

- Live in obedience to God's will as laid out in His Word.

- Live a life of purity.

- Pray for your future spouse.

- Do good to your future spouse even now.

Let's talk about that last one for a moment. I love these verses in Proverbs 31 about the virtuous woman:

"A wife of noble character who can find?
She is worth far more than rubies.
Her husband has full confidence in her
And lacks nothing of value.
She brings him good, not harm,
All the days of her life."[8] [emphasis mine]

Notice that this woman is bringing her husband good not just from the moment they met, not just from the day of their wedding. No, she is doing her husband good ALL the days of her life.

Friend, this means that even in your singleness, you can do good to your future husband or wife. Do your best to live a holy life, one above reproach. Remember the value of purity and wait for your spouse. Pray for him or her. Do good to him even before you know him. Be a blessing to her before you even meet.

Waiting can be hard. But your peace, your happiness and your future depend on your ability to wait. Don't ever forget that God is faithful and He will be faithful to you. "Let us hold unswervingly to the hope we profess, for he who promised is faithful" (Hebrews 10:23).

In the next chapter, we'll talk about what you may be looking for in a future spouse. It is important to be considering these things now.

Chatter At The Well

What if I'm supposed to be single?

I do believe there are individuals whom God calls to singleness. Often, this discovery is made over time with much prayer and reflection on the matter. With singleness comes more opportunity to focus on the Lord, serve Him and give undivided attention to ministry opportunities simply because there are less distractions. When I was single, it was much easier to serve in ministry work because I didn't have the responsibility of a husband and children. Are you called to a life of singleness? Only God will reveal that. But I can tell you that if God's plan is for you to remain single, you will find satisfaction, fulfillment and joy in that which He calls you. He will provide you with grace after grace for each task. And whether He calls you to be single for a time or indefinitely, it doesn't change your responsibility in this season: Serve and follow hard after Him.

"Trust in the Lord with all of your heart and lean not on your own understanding. In all your ways acknowledge him and he will make your paths straight." Proverbs 3:5-6

More Than Tall,
Dark and Handsome

Chapter Four

AFTER COLLEGE, I MOVED BACK home with my mom and took a job in my hometown. The job wasn't in my field of study, but I knew the Lord was leading me there. It is rather humbling to come out of four years of college and take a job that isn't at all related to the courses you studied. But when the Lord leads, you follow. And it was a great place to work with many blessings I could never have imagined.

During this time, I found a wonderful group of girlfriends and we would hang out and encourage each other. I traveled to Pittsburgh frequently to visit Tara, my dear friend from college. And I also became involved in a women's Bible study group at church. I was the youngest by probably 20 years but I loved those women. I learned from them, prayed with them and grew so much in the

Lord during that time. This special group of ladies never questioned me on why I was single or pressured me to settle down and get married. They just loved on me.

One day, my mom came home from a hair appointment and told me that the owner of the salon asked if she could set me up on a blind date. To tell you the truth, I was initially indignant toward the idea of a blind date. Not only did I not want to go out with a complete stranger (hello stranger danger!), but I didn't know anything about this guy. What was he like? Was he a nice person? Was he even a believer?

My mom explained a bit more. Lydia, the salon owner, had stopped my mom to ask if I would go out on a date with her cousin. Knowing how important faith was to me, my mom hesitantly asked if he was a Christian. To which Lydia replied, "Oh, yes."

Even with that knowledge, it still didn't sound like a good idea. I ran a quick errand, which apparently gave the Lord enough time to work on my heart. I came home and somewhat reluctantly agreed.

Within a few days, Dan was leaving a message on the house answering machine. (Yes, people still had landlines back then.) We connected and made a date for coffee . . . learning later that neither of us actually like a cup of joe. Before we met, I prayed and I wondered if this guy would match up with the things I was looking for in a husband. What was his relationship with the Lord like? What things did he value? Was he kind? Did he stand up for what was right?

When Abraham's servant prayed and asked that God would give him success, laying out his request for the sign of the right girl, what we don't read in the passage is what qualities Eliezer was looking for in a bride for Isaac. But a little thought and investigation is all that is needed to reveal his holy agenda.

Eliezer prayed that when he asked a girl for water, the right one, the one chosen by God, would also offer to get water for his camels. Now, let's remember the fact that Eliezer took 10 camels with him on his journey. Each camel could drink 25 gallons of water.[9] That is a lot of water and a lot of work!

The servant of Abraham was looking for someone with a servant's heart, a strong work ethic, simple courtesy and kindness. Later in our story, we will also see that Rebekah is hospitable, modest and willing to follow the Lord's leading.

What is it that you desire in a spouse? What is most important to you? Take a few moments and think about what you value. Do you want someone with a generous heart, integrity . . . maybe someone you can laugh with?

What are things you do not want? Maybe you have dated someone before who didn't value family and now, you recognize how important that is to you. Do you want someone with strong morals and this is something on which you won't compromise? Are there certain characteristics or qualities that you know you do not want in a marriage partner?

I can't stress enough this little exercise of thinking through what it is you want and do not want in a future spouse. Knowing this ahead of time can save you so much grief and it will help you not to settle for less.

In that first job out of college, I remember being told by a lady I worked with that my standards were too high and that I was being too picky. I had turned down a delivery guy asking me out on a date. With the little that I did know about him, I knew it wouldn't be a match. There were some pretty big differences and quite honestly, I didn't want to waste my time . . . or his for that matter. I knew I wanted to start on the common ground of faith and values. I also knew the Lord had chosen someone for me and that there would be certain things we had in common.

When you are choosing to wait at the well and not hop on every opportunity to go on a date, you will find blessing. Can you go on dates? Absolutely. But don't waste your time getting entangled in relationships with which there is no future.

How do you decide if there is a future? Look to God's Word and your most valued traits in a future spouse. Don't settle for less. You're a child of the King and He takes care of His children. Proverbs 19:14 reminds us that a good wife is from the Lord. He will provide.

So what are examples of character traits to look for?

When I was single, there were many traits I wanted in the person I would marry, and these qualities were so much more than tall, dark and handsome. Here were some of them:

- A believer who loved the Lord (more on this later)

- A kind and servant's heart

- Integrity and honesty

- Trustworthy

- Hardworking

- Makes good decisions

- Treats me well

- Strong character

- Love of family

- Sense of humor

These were things that I especially valued. But your list may have more. Look back at Rebekah. One scholar refers to her humility, industrious nature, willingness to work, courteous disposition and charity toward strangers. She responds to an opportunity to do good.[10] Another highlights "her beauty, courteous kindness, willing consent and modesty."[11] She sounds like a lovely person. She wasn't some crude, provocative, angry woman. No, she had character. She had heart.

If you have a moment, take a more detailed look at the woman in Proverbs 31. She, too, is a woman of character. She is of great worth to her husband. (Ladies, don't you want to be of great worth to the man you marry?) Her husband has confidence in her. She is referred to as a helper, a hard worker and an early riser (don't worry if this isn't you!). She considers her options before making a decision; she is strong. She is well prepared and takes care of her family. She is giving and thoughtful to those in need. She does not worry. She is wise and counsels others with faithful instruction. She is not idle. She is admired by her children and husband. She fears the Lord.

Now ladies, you may be thinking, "Whoosh! She is amazing. How can I match up to that?" Think of this not as a checklist, but as something to inspire you to be better. But certainly for all of us (men, too), we can look at this list of qualities and fine tune what it is that we value in a potential mate.

Now is anyone going to have all the qualities we've touched on? No. Most definitely not. None of us are perfect and we are all still growing. Think of what you want most and trust God to bring you the right person. And let me tell you, if you are a child of God, the right person will always have one particular quality. If the person does not have this quality, I can promise you that they are not the right person or it isn't the right time to pursue love with them. This is so important that . . . well, I've given it its own chapter.

What You May Not Want to Hear

Chapter Five

I AM SO GLAD YOU'RE staying with me because this journey just wouldn't be as much fun without you. Let's take a quick glance back to the very beginning of our story. We will see that Abraham places a very specific demand when it comes to looking for a wife for his son, Isaac.

> Abraham was now very old, and the Lord had blessed him in every way. He said to the senior servant in his household, the one in charge of all that he had, "Put your hand under my thigh. I want you to swear by the Lord, the God of heaven and the God of earth, that you will not get a wife for my son from the daughters of the Canaanites, among whom I am living, but will go to my country and my own relatives and get a wife for my son Isaac." (Genesis 24:1-4)

Now, I am about to step on some of your toes and I will try do it with the most grace and gentleness as possible. The risk of you closing the book after this chapter is one I am willing to take because this is the particular quality I spoke about in the last chapter and the single most important thing to look for in a spouse. Your decision to make this a priority will affect the rest of your life. It is crucial to the growth of your faith and future joy. You should also know that we are about to get to some of the best parts of this love story and I would hate for you to miss it.

What is this big request that Abraham requires of Eliezer in looking for a wife for Isaac? What does Abraham make him promise? Abraham stipulates that Eliezer not find a wife among the Canaanites, but rather go back to Abraham's home country and find a woman there. Why is this important? Because the Canaanites were wicked idolaters who worshipped false gods, not the one true God. Abraham wanted someone of like-faith for his son.

Have you ever heard a Christian talk about being equally yoked? 2 Corinthians 6:14 says, "Do not be yoked together with unbelievers." Let's dig into this concept a little.

In agriculture, a farmer may put two oxen side by side with a yoke to accomplish a particular task. It may be to plow a field, move a heavy load or another sort of job. A yoke is the harness that goes around their necks and connects the two oxen together. Do a quick Google search for some images and you'll see exactly what I mean. The yoke helps the animals to work a job simultaneously. It allows them to work together. One purpose. One passion. One focus.

If the oxen are not the same size (hence the term unequally yoked), they will try to move at different speeds and different rhythms, and will not be able to work well together. In some cases, they won't be able to walk straight because the tension between the animals is too great. "The result would be an inability to cooperate, would likely result in conflict between the animals, perhaps damaging the valuable yoke or even injuring the animals."[12]

Deuteronomy 22:10 instructs the farmers not to plow with an ox and a donkey yoked together. Can you picture two different animals trying to pull a load? Would it be efficient? Would it be without struggle? Would it be fun?

The practicality of this principle for the believer is great. If you are a follower of Christ and you marry someone who is not a believer, you are setting yourself up for struggle. Not only does God instruct His children to be equally yoked in marriage, but there also exists many pragmatic reasons for marrying someone who is like-minded as well.

If you are not equally yoked, how will you and your spouse handle different situations that arise? Your responses to life's challenges could be quite different than that of your spouse. How will you handle going to church? Where will you turn when there are hard times? How will you raise your children? What happens when your children are growing in their faith and the unbelieving spouse starts to resent what they are being taught? I cannot tell you enough how this will pervade EVERY AREA of your lives as a married couple.

Please don't see this as a snobby approach to dating and marriage. Rather see it as God's protective advice not only from the spiritual side of growing your faith, but also the most practical side . . . where the rubber meets the road in daily living.

Take a look: The coupled partnered in faith will be one united front with the decision to follow and seek God and abide by His Word, the Bible. An unequally yoked couple will likely differ in the way they make decisions, handle money, raise their children and spend their time.

Do you pray about big decisions? What will the differences be here? You may want to follow where you believe God is leading. Don't expect the non-believing partner to follow along.

One partner may not want to tithe whereas the Bible-believing partner will want to give 10 percent of the family income to his or her church. The unbelieving spouse may see money as all his or hers with no need to follow any biblical directive. The Christian views him or herself as a steward (or manager) in the way money is handled.

An unequally yoked couple will struggle in the way they raise and teach their children. When I think of how many conversations we have had with our kids about the daily challenges of living in this world, our belief in God, the authority of the Bible and salvation through Jesus, our faith is the single most integral foundation of all our teaching.

As a believer, I want my kids to be raised in the faith. What kind of example would an unbelieving husband be to my son? He would not show my son how to be a strong man of God, how to weather the storms of life with prayer, devotion and faith. If this is important to you, then you need to marry a believer. If you want a wife who will demonstrate the beauty of godly living to a little girl, then you need to marry a believer. Think about the kind of environment in which you would want children to be raised.

Maddie was a young Christian adult who fell in love with a nice guy named Michael. They were a cute couple however, Michael didn't value faith or the church life that Maddie grew up with. While their love continued to grow, Maddie continued to ignore that nagging feeling regarding the lack of Michael's faith. Secretly, she just hoped he would come to know the Lord as time went on. After all, she was deeply in love with him.

What she didn't take notice of was that this relationship with Michael was a drain on her relationship with the Lord. She no longer felt the fire that once burned within her. Her devotional times became less and less until they were pretty much non-existent.

Time went on and Michael proposed. Maddie was beyond thrilled. She began planning the wedding of her dreams. The two "M's" would look so cute on well . . . everything. Michael attended church with Maddie on occasion and Maddie continued to hope that he would become more interested in the things of God.

But it didn't happen. They married, went to church rather infrequently until Maddie became pregnant. Something happens when you start a family. Individuals raised in the church often want to return as they remember the value of being involved in a community of faith.

The unfortunate part was that Michael had no desire to raise his family in Christianity. He wasn't just disinterested in church life, he was opposed to teaching his children something he personally did not believe. As their family grew, it caused more and more dissension when Maddie tried to take her children to church that she finally gave up. The arguments were too many. The conflict was too great. There was no explaining to Michael how important her faith was because Michael never saw the importance before. All he could say was that she changed and it felt unfair.

If you marry an unbeliever, let me ask you: How will you run the race together? How will you challenge each other to grow closer to God? This is His plan for marriage. If your faith is important to you, wouldn't you *want* to spend your life with someone who has the same core beliefs?

Now, let's take it a step further. I am going to tell you something that will save your heart so much grief and pain. Don't get romantically involved with someone who is not a Christian . . . and for some of you who have trouble guarding your heart that means only date Christians.

I know there are many of you throwing up your arms right now in the disbelief of my snobbiness (is that even a word?). But being snobby has absolutely nothing do with it.

Let's think about it this way. Will the person you one day marry be someone you have dated and with whom you've fallen in love? The answer is obviously, yes. We don't live in a time of arranged marriages. You will have dated and grown to love the individual you will be marrying.

Now, if you date a non-Christian, how will you protect your heart from falling in love? Biblically speaking, you can't marry this person. How will you keep yourself (and this other person) from falling in love and giving your heart? My niece calls it a slippery slope, one that is very hard to maintain safe footing.

Oh, I know some of you are thinking that you can handle it. You are thinking you can keep this all above board and not get too entangled. You won't think long term, (and by the way guys, that girl is usually thinking long term even if she says she isn't). It is either this or you are holding out secret hope that they will come to know the Lord while you are dating. And yes, there is always hope. But hoping through a dating relationship that someone will come to faith is not the way. You are not spurring each other on in faith at this critical part of your relationship.

Let me tell you about another couple.

Lydia was a strong, single Christian in her mid-thirties. She was interested in meeting someone so she joined the dating website, eHarmony, that touts itself as being able to match compatible individuals. You should first know that Lydia was committed to marrying a Christian. She knew what the Bible said about being equally yoked. But she had also seen the challenge and impact in other families when a believer married an unbeliever. There would be no compromising for her on this.

Lydia was very open about her faith in her eHarmony profile. She put "Baptist" in the religion area and specifically mentioned that her faith was important to her in the notes. So when she was matched with Brent, who listed himself as a Buddhist/Taoist, Lydia thought eHarmony's algorithm was tanked. Lydia was not even going to respond, but Brent reached out through eHarmony's instant messenger and they ended up chatting online and on the phone for a couple of weeks.

Brent seemed like a very nice guy. He was polite, respectful and not at all like some of the creeps Lydia had gone out with before. But he wasn't a Christian. He was a Buddhist with a master's degree in theological studies and a doctorate in religion who had even travelled all the way to Thailand and India to learn more about native religions.

All through the process, Lydia was forthcoming about her Christian faith and the fact that there was no future because of their differences on this matter. Yet, Brent kept pursuing getting to know Lydia better. They met in person, to which Lydia took along her cousin, Hannah. Now, if you had met Lydia and thought she was bold, Hannah takes it to a whole new level. At the first opportunity that night, Hannah questioned Brent about matters of faith. She was kind, yet to the point.

As Lydia and Brent casually got to know each other, Lydia guarded her heart. She did not allow herself to become romantically interested in Brent. She simply didn't want to get to that uncomfortable place in a relationship where she either had to compromise her beliefs because she was so in love or break up for the very reason she knew all along wouldn't allow her to marry him.

Guarding your heart can be such a hard thing to do, but by keeping it black and white with the future in mind, she was able to do it. After a few weeks, they both decided their friendship wasn't leading to anything more, so they cut it off. But what happened next was nothing short of a move of God and a blessing for Lydia in her obedience.

Shortly after, Brent began calling her again. He had questions about Lydia's faith. You see, Brent was attracted to the peaceful nature of Buddhism, but he had never felt peace. He saw Lydia's complete peace paired with zero doubt about her faith in Christ and he was intrigued.

That was when the long phone conversations started. Hours and hours talking about faith. Brent drilling her with question after question. Lydia was exhausted. Yet the Lord helped her answer each question, explain all doubts and resolve every concern. She would be up to all hours of the night talking on the phone about salvation, Jesus, the Bible and so much more.

Still Lydia held no romantic feelings for Brent. She only knew she couldn't shut the door on someone asking questions about faith. Through those conversations, the Lord was at work on Brent's heart. And quickly, Brent came to faith in Jesus. True faith. True profession. True peace.

Lydia had been careful during this process to tell Brent not to claim Christianity because of her. That can always be a concern for a believer that someone will jump on board to aid the relationship in moving forward. However, this was not the case at all. And love didn't happen for Lydia right away, either.

It wasn't until a few months later that Lydia began to realize she had feelings for this former Buddhist turned Christian. And, if you want to know the end of the story, they got married! Lydia's resolve to guard her heart and wait on the Lord worked out in the most amazing way. True love with a believer was worth the wait!

This is what Brent had to say on the matter.

> When Lydia and I were getting to know each other, we got along on so many levels . . . except faith. I was learned in all the philosophies of man and had been on a self-professed search for Truth for 20 years. The chances for Lydia to have convinced or convicted me on her own were almost zero. I experienced a peace around her, and her certainty exceeded the value of my familiarity with numerous philosophies. It was all the work of the Spirit which coordinated a most unlikely series of events as part of God's plan. Lydia never wavered from her faith despite my most sophisticated of questions. As I reflect on it again, it was truly amazing. To this day, when I describe my conversion to non-Christian intellectuals I talk about how peace of faith supersedes all possible human knowledge. God is too immense to be understood by any man—what folly! The peace of faith so transformed my life that nothing else I've experienced or studied could even begin to compare. It was beautiful, first God loved me and gifted me salvation, then Lydia and I fell in love.

It is completely okay to pursue friendship with a non-Christian. It is a whole different animal to pursue a dating relationship with someone who does not share your faith beliefs. It is far too easy to fall in love and way too hard to walk away. Do yourself and the other person a favor, don't date someone you wouldn't actually marry.

For the last twenty years, I have seen couples in this situation. Some have made the hard choice and not without great heartache, broken up with the individual because the believer realized he or she could not marry this person. But I have also seen individuals proceed and go through with marriage. They then live with the difficulty of being with someone who doesn't prioritize the things of God in his or her life.

An unequally yoked relationship keeps you from moving in the same direction, at the same speed and at the same rhythm. What is it you want for your life? Wait for the one God has chosen for you. Wait.

"Unless the Lord builds the house,
the builders labor in vain." Psalm 127:1

When Waiting is H.A.R.D.

Chapter Six

SO WE HAVE TALKED ABOUT looking for the right kind of person, we have explored the idea of God preparing you and your future mate for each other, but what about when waiting is just plain hard?

Last Friday, we were driving to Cedar Point for the weekend. If you are a thrill-seeking, roller coaster-loving kind of person and have not yet visited this amusement park in northwestern Ohio, then I'd suggest you plan a trip. With multiple record-breaking roller coasters pushing you to amazing and crazy limits . . . well my husband does them all. I only do the ones that don't make me want to vomit. Enough said.

We were heading to Cedar Point for a blogging conference I was attending. My family loves this because I go to sessions and they get to hit the park. It makes for a fun weekend for the whole family. We had planned on leaving right from the kids' school in order to arrive at our hotel during the conference registration window. However, not taking into account construction and the fun of rush hour in downtown Cleveland, I became quite nervous about getting there in time. A late arrival meant no early registration. No early registration meant no park tickets for the evening and I had been so looking forward to riding some new coasters with my daughter who met another height requirement for more rides.

Now, usually I don't mind going slow in traffic. I'd pick slow over crazy driving any day. However, my anxiety over being late was growing and I was admittedly starting to stress. Looking down the highway with my hands tightly grasping the steering wheel, I knew our speed was not going to increase any time soon. So I did what anyone in this situation does, change lanes to try to go faster.

But low and behold, I found myself behind a big, white box truck going around dead-man's curve (they call it that for a reason). Traffic was full and tight across four lanes. There was no moving around at this point. So I stayed behind the big truck. I could see nothing ahead of me. All I could frustratingly notice were the cars flying by me on both sides. They were all moving ahead and there I was stuck having to wait, moving slowly behind this gigantic white box on wheels. My only path was to trust the fact that I was going in the right direction no matter what my speed.

Waiting can be hard. There may be times when you see all your friends flying by, getting engaged . . . getting married. It may seem like everyone is being matched up and you're stuck behind this big white box truck.

But let me encourage you: It may be difficult. It may be lonely. But if you are waiting for the one God has for you, it will be worth the wait. God is faithful. Wait for His timing.

I will confess that I didn't find the waiting too difficult. I had surely hoped that I would find someone sooner than later, but I was somehow able to find the grace to get through that time and many of my friends were still single as well. That can make a big difference. But for Dan, my husband, the waiting was more challenging. His friends and family were getting married and he longed for companionship. But even after we met, despite both wanting to get married, we were not going to jump on board unless we knew the Lord was leading us to one another in marriage.

Marriage has its own set of challenges. If you've ever heard someone say that marriage is hard work, they were telling the truth. You've got two sinners with different upbringings, different personalities and different ways of doing things. I mean seriously, wait until your spouse puts the toilet paper on the wrong way or leaves the kitchen a mess and you're a neat freak. Of course, there will be natural bumps on the road.

But as bigger issues arise, life and the working through of those circumstances will be much smoother if you have started your marriage at the well, running the same race and with a common purpose, knowing that the Lord has brought you together.

Persevere in waiting. There's no need to rush.

The Right Kind vs. The Right One Debate

Here comes the tough question on which many Christians think differently. Some believe there is a right ONE person for you to marry and others believe you only need to look for the right KIND of person.

I make my tent in the first camp. However, I don't have a problem if you are looking for the right kind of person. Good for you. You have decided on important qualities and characteristics that would make for a good spouse and line up with your personality.

But you still need to seek God on whether you should marry that person. Here is the way I think about it. When I would pray if a particular guy was the person that God had for me, it was done with several underlying premises:

- God is omniscient (all-knowing).

- He knows me better than I know myself.

- He knows that other person equally as well.

- He cares about every aspect of my life.

- God is a God of details.

- God is for me not against me.

- He reveals His will and speaks to His children.

- He gives wisdom when asked.

- He would never lead me outside of His perfect will if I am seeking and submitting.

- The blessing of my relationship would be maximized in following His leading.

- Therefore, I wanted the person that God has given to me to marry.

Sure, we can get hairy and ponder things like if that person dies and then God brings you another, then there wasn't just one person. Well, that is true. God has blessed you with another mate to marry.

I love the conversation that Henry, the prince, and Leonardo da Vinci have in the movie, *Ever After*.[13] The movie is an adaption of the Cinderella story and Henry is confused about who he is supposed to be with. In the movie, Leonardo da Vinci plays a mentoring role to the baffled prince.

Henry says, "Do you really think there is only one perfect mate?"

"As a matter of fact, I do." replies Leonardo.

"Well then how can you be certain to find them? And if you do find them, are they really the one for you or do you only think they are? And what happens if the person you're supposed to be with never appears or . . . or she does, but you're too distracted to notice?"

"You learn to pay attention."

"Then let's say God puts two people on Earth and they are lucky enough to find one another. But one of them gets hit by lightning. Well then what? Is that it? Or, perchance, you meet someone new and marry all over again. Is that the lady you're supposed to be with or was it the first? And if so, when the two of them were walking side by side were they both the one for you and you just happened to meet the first one first or, was the second one supposed to be first? And is everything just chance or are some things meant to be?"

Just as it was for Henry, sometimes it can feel like there is so much noise and confusion when trying to figure out if someone is the right person. But all that is needed is waiting on the Lord and seeking His will. Be patient. Be confident that He reveals what His children need to know. For anyone and on any important issue, you will NEVER go wrong in seeking God, waiting on Him and submitting to His will over your own.

Could I have married the guy I dated before Dan? Sure. It probably would have been a fine marriage. Would it have been great? I don't know. But I do know that by seeking God and following His lead, I found the most wonderful guy who is my match in so many more ways. I have every confidence in God's leading me to him and I feel the pleasure and blessing of the Lord as this man's wife. He was worth waiting for!

We're finally to the point of God revealing His will in the account of Isaac and Rebekah. And that is what we'll discover next.

Part Four
Meeting at the Well

Before He Even Finished

Chapter Seven

A H, THE STORY IS ABOUT to get good! We'll see how God answers Eliezer's request, who He answers with and the result of His answer. Let's dive back in . . .

> Before he had finished praying, Rebekah came out with her jar on her shoulder. She was the daughter of Bethuel son of Milkah, who was the wife of Abraham's brother Nahor. The woman was very beautiful, a virgin; no man had ever slept with her. She went down to the spring, filled her jar and came up again. (Genesis 24:15-16)

When we last left Eliezer, he was knee deep in prayer asking the Lord for success on behalf of his master for his quest of finding a wife for Isaac. Notice what verse 15 says, "Before he had finished praying, Rebekah came out . . . ." Isn't that just awesome?

God may not always bring about an answer for us in meeting our spouses so quickly (for a variety of good reasons), but this is an incredible principle to remember when we are praying for other things. There will be those glorious times when you are praying in line with the heart of God, for the success of your quest and before you even finish, God has moved mightily and answered your prayer.

After Dan and I had dated for a while and sought the Lord, we arrived at the conclusion that the Lord was leading us to a life together. We knew that much. What Dan wasn't too sure about was the timing for getting married. He didn't know how fast to move or if we were supposed to wait longer and continue dating.

One morning, he sat at his bedroom desk and prayed . . . seeking the Lord for direction and guidance as to the future timing of our relationship. He had started looking at engagement rings and had found one in particular he liked. But still he sought the Lord.

Later that same morning at work, Dan was called to the office of the president of the company. He didn't know why and this wasn't something that happened . . . ever. Dan stepped into the office and the president handed Dan a check. The president (who wasn't the jolliest kind of guy) told Dan not to expect this every year. It was a discretionary bonus and would not be repeated during

Dan's 10 years at that job. Not only was this the first bonus Dan had ever received from this company, but it was also the entire amount of the ring he wanted to buy. The Lord had quickly answered his request for direction. You can probably imagine Dan's excitement and joy. Unfortunately at the time, he couldn't share any of this with me because he wanted the proposal to be a surprise. But nonetheless, God had answered Dan's prayer clearly and quickly.

Let's take a look at what happens next when Eliezer speaks to Rebekah.

> The servant hurried to meet her and said, "Please give me a little water from your jar."
>
> "Drink, my lord," she said, and quickly lowered the jar to her hands and gave him a drink.
>
> After she had given him a drink, she said, "I'll draw water for your camels too, until they have had enough to drink." So she quickly emptied her jar into the trough, ran back to the well to draw more water, and drew enough for all his camels. Without saying a word, the man watched her closely to learn whether or not the Lord had made his journey successful. (Genesis 24:17-21)

What do you think about our Rebekah? She was quick to lower her jar and give this old servant a drink. How kind that was of her. But then notice she goes further by offering to draw water for the camels and runs back to the well to draw more. Now, aside from the fact that I do not run (let's just say I look ridiculous when I run but lower back issues also prevent me from doing so), I don't know that I would be rushing to draw water for 10 camels when each can drink so much! How about you?

I love what Eliezer does next. "Without saying a word, the man watched her closely to learn whether or not the Lord had made his journey successful."

Without saying a word . . . he observed. He evaluated. His eyes were peeled to see if this was the one the Lord had chosen.

> When the camels had finished drinking, the man took out a gold nose ring weighing a beka and two gold bracelets weighing ten shekels. Then he asked, "Whose daughter are you? Please tell me, is there room in your father's house for us to spend the night?"
>
> She answered him, "I am the daughter of Bethuel, the son that Milkah bore to Nahor." And she added, "We have plenty of straw and fodder, as well as room for you to spend the night." (Genesis 24:22-25)

I don't know how long it takes a camel to drink, but with 10 camels capable of drinking up to 25 gallons and having to go back and forth to draw water, I am imagining that Abraham's servant sat for quite a while. Our passage tells us that when the camels had finished drinking, Eliezer gave Rebekah the jewelry and then asked if there was room for him at her father's house.

Now, if you aren't up on Abraham's genealogy, it would be helpful to know that Nahor was Abraham's brother. Bethuel was Nahor's son and Rebekah's father. So relatively speaking, Rebekah is Abraham's great niece.

Don't forget that part of Eliezer's task was to find Isaac's wife from among his people and not from the Canaanites. Was this just a coincidence that Rebekah was the one Eliezer found? No sir! It was the appointment of God at the right time and at the right place.

Rebekah then offers a place to stay for Eliezer, his companions and his camels. Here we learn another one of Rebekah's character traits. She is not only kind, but she is also hospitable.

> Then the man bowed down and worshiped the Lord, saying, "Praise be to the Lord, the God of my master Abraham, who has not abandoned his kindness and faithfulness to my master. As for me, the Lord has led me on the journey to the house of my master's relatives." (Genesis 24:26-27)

The Lord did not just answer Eliezer's prayer quickly and with a wonderful girl, He specifically answered with someone from among Abraham's relatives. I can only imagine how joyful Eliezer must have immediately felt when discovering the identity of this camel-waterer.

Take notice of what the Scripture records as his response: worship. Abraham's servant bows down and worships the Lord. When you have gone to the well, prayed and waited on God, and then found the one to whom He has led you, the most appropriate, the most beautiful, the deepest inclination of your heart should be to bow down and worship the Most High. Once I knew that the Lord had led me to Dan, all I could do was ooze worship for the Lord. His blessing was overwhelming. I had to praise Him. I was humbled at His kindness, His favor and His interest in my life.

And even Rebekah knows something good is up. Look at her next action.

> The young woman ran and told her mother's household about these things. (Genesis 24:28)

Oh, how I love her! I am looking forward to the day that my kids run home and tell me all about how the Lord is moving in such a way in their lives. And as we talk about all that is going on, I know Dan and I will have many things to tell them. Curious what we'll say? Read on, my friend.

Chatter At The Well

So often I meet someone who says he or she is a Christian, but his or her life and actions do not reflect this. How can I meet someone who really loves the Lord? I'm not getting any younger!

I know there are times when you may feel that you will never meet your future spouse. It can be hard and lonely. And you may have already been waiting a long time. You need to remember how big your God is. The One who parted the Red Sea, caused the walls of Jericho to fall at a shout, created the heavens and the earth, He who healed the lame, who died yet returned to life . . . He can surely bring about an introduction with someone who loves the Lord as you do. He will not forget, nor has He forgotten you. Continue to trust Him. You need only to seek Him with your whole heart and wait on Him for the right time.

"Wait for the Lord; be strong and take heart and wait for the Lord." Psalm 27:14

". . . being confident of this, that he who began a good work in you will carry it on to completion until the day of Christ Jesus." Philippians 1:6

Around my Kitchen Table

Chapter Eight

WHEN YOU HAVE MET SOMEONE and started dating, how I wish we could sit down around my kitchen table for a chat. For the ladies, we'd enjoy a cup of loose leaf tea and assorted tea cookies. I'd make them look all pretty on tiered white cake plates. For the guys, well, I'd make you something with meat . . . probably my awesome meatball subs. The meatball recipe is from Disney World, which makes it especially delicious. What would we talk about? If nothing else, we'd talk about four things.

Prayer

When you are starting to date someone, be like Eliezer and pray. Pray for direction, for guidance. Pray that your heart will be guarded. Pray for wisdom and discernment. Pray for God to reveal truth. I am of the mind that you would rather find out now if the person is not right for you rather than wasting months, even years on someone with whom you have no future.

Read this:

> My son, if you accept my words and store up my commands within you, turning your ear to wisdom and applying your heart to understanding—indeed, if you call out for insight and cry aloud for understanding, and if you look for it as for silver and search for it as for hidden treasure, then you will understand the fear of the Lord and find the knowledge of God. For the Lord gives wisdom; from his mouth come knowledge and understanding. He holds success in store for the upright, he is a shield to those whose walk is blameless, for he guards the course of the just and protects the way of his faithful ones. Then you will understand what is right and just and fair—every good path. For wisdom will enter your heart, and knowledge will be pleasant to your soul. (Proverbs 2:1-10)

Isn't this a wonderful nugget from God's word? If you ask for wisdom, if you ask for direction, God will give it to you. You will understand every good path.

A verse I will often share or pray over someone seeking direction is from Isaiah 30:21 and this is my prayer for you. "Whether you turn to the right or to the left, your ears will hear a voice behind you, saying, 'This is the way;

walk in it.'" I pray that the Lord will speak clearly to you and show you the way you should walk.

Guarding Your Heart

Do you ever wonder why Christians say to guard your heart? Proverbs 4:23 says "Above all else, guard your heart, for it is the wellspring of life."14 In romantic relationships, guarding your heart really is just a fancy way of saying don't fall in love too quickly.

The excitement of a new relationship can be fun, but your brain needs to stay engaged. It is easy to fall in love and let's face it, sometimes when you are in that stage of infatuation, you aren't seeing everything as it really is.

Am I saying that Christians shouldn't feel this ooey gooey kind of love? Absolutely not! All I am saying is don't jump into the pool with your eyes completely closed. Keep some perspective, pray and guard your heart.

Willing Submission

Then after we poured another cup of tea or melted the cheese on a second meatball sub, we would talk about submission. Submission is putting the will and authority of another before your own. It is submitting or yielding to someone or something else. In this case, we are talking about submission to God.

Now, if the Most High God were some mean, grumpy, uncaring dictator, this would be completely unenticing. However, the God we serve is loving, caring and wholly interested in the details of our lives. He is for us and not against us. He always has our best in mind. Even though we may find it hard at times to give up what we want, submission to a loving God should really be an easy choice.

After Dan and I had been married for a year, he was approached with a new job opportunity at a different company. He had been at the current job for 10 years and loved it there. His co-workers had become family and he is not one to be excited about big change. However, the person who reached out to him had been a previous boss and was a man that Dan admired, respected and trusted. He agreed to meet out of politeness to this man because truly, he had no desire to change jobs.

When that meeting led to further phone conversations and dinners to meet other employees at the company, Dan began to feel quite torn. He saw the pros and cons with both choices (staying at the current job/changing to a new job). He didn't know what to do. The one thing he could do was seek God. Dan trusted that the Lord would provide the right direction. And while his heart was conflicted at times, he trusted the One who saw the big picture and loved him.

For weeks, we longed for an answer. Our desperate prayer for direction became based on Psalm 40:8, "I desire to do your will." Here is what we prayed:

Lord, we don't know what is best.
We desire to do Your will.

Lord, You know the future You have for us.
We desire to do Your will.

Lord, You know Dan and his skill set best.
We desire to do Your will.

Lord, You know the heartache of leaving a
company and the friends who are like family.
But we desire to do Your will.

Lord, You know how hard it is to change
jobs and move to the unknown.
But we desire to do Your will.

Lord, guide us as You see fit because
we desire to do Your will.

Now, I had a feeling that this new job was indeed the hand of the Lord. But Dan needed to know that too. He was the one who had to pick up and leave when he didn't really want to.

Submission means yielding to God's desire for your life, even your love life. It is putting what He wants for you above what (or who) you may want for yourself. In all areas of life, it is the path of the believer: trusting a guide who will lead you around the next bend in the road even when the road remains for you unseen.

The Lord thoroughly knows you and the person you are dating. Trust Him. Seek Him. Make a decision to yield to what He knows is best for you. Incidentally, Dan took the new job and has been there for over 10 years. It was totally the right move but Dan wouldn't have seen that beforehand if he hadn't been seeking the Lord and been willing to submit.

Seeking the Counsel of Others

The final thing we would talk about is seeking the counsel of others. In Proverbs 12:15, the Bible tells us, "The way of fools seems right to them, but the wise listen to advice."

As you are considering the future of your relationship, talk to godly couples. Talk to your pastor, teachers and leaders in your church. Ask your parents what they think. Keep in mind how well your parents know you. Get their take on your relationship and the person you are dating.

When Rebekah's father, Bethuel, and brother, Laban, had heard all that Eliezer said, look at their response.

Laban and Bethuel answered, "This is from the Lord; we can say nothing to you one way or the other. Here is Rebekah; take her and go, and let her become the wife of your master's son, as the Lord has directed." (Genesis 24:50-51)

There is a very good chance your parents have been praying for your future spouse for quite a while. Ask them what they think. Listen to any of their concerns. Don't get upset or frustrated with any negative opinions. Take it all in so that you can properly evaluate the person you are dating and the potential future of the relationship. And that is what we're talking about in the next chapter!

Chatter At The Well

No one believes in abstinence before marriage anymore. Is it still important? I can't tell you how many couples I know who are living together.

Even though pre-marital sex and cohabitation are completely common and considered normal in our culture, I can tell you that the Bible has not changed. God still values purity, holiness and not giving even the appearance of sin. God intended your purity to be a gift for your future spouse. Sex outside of marriage, just like other sin, not only hurts

---

your relationship with God, but you are also forming a bond with that person without the covering and life-long commitment that God has created in marriage.

Now, I am not so naive to believe that every person reading this book has made a commitment to wait until marriage. However if you decide now to make that commitment, I can tell you that you will find forgiveness and healing in Christ. Repercussions may still exist and you will have to share that with the one you hope to marry, but the Lord can restore you. Make a fresh commitment and wait.

"Therefore, I urge you, brothers and sisters, in view of God's mercy, to offer your bodies as a living sacrifice, holy and pleasing to God—this is your true and proper worship. Do not conform to the pattern of this world, but be transformed by the renewing of your mind. Then you will be able to test and approve what God's will is—his good, pleasing and perfect will." Romans 12:1-2

Time To Evaluate

Chapter Nine

FOR THE LAST FIVE YEARS, Dan and I have taught our church's Sunday School class for high school students. For a period of about three of those years, the college-aged students also joined us every Sunday morning. We have covered many fun and challenging topics in those years over strong, student-made coffee, asiago cheese bagels and a single shared toaster that apparently and most recently caused quite a stir in the church as concerned individuals searched all over for the strong burning smell in the building. Yep, that's our class. Want to join? Follow the odor of well-toasted carbs.

At the moment, we are working through Dave Ramsey's *Foundations*. (It is basically the student version of Financial Peace University.) I love teaching on God's way of handling money. But once again like so many of our other topics, it has elicited a conversation on marriage and evaluating a dating relationship.

The person you share a bank account with may not have the same spending, saving and giving habits you do. Maybe they are better at handling money (hooray!) or maybe they are worse (uh-oh!). Money can be a great source of conflict in marriage if you and your mate aren't on the same page in how you handle it. In fact, it is commonly recognized as a leading cause of divorce.

Dan has repeatedly told our students, in this study and over the many years, that there were two major things he considered when dating a girl other than her faith. He asked himself first if she would be a good mother to children. Dan knew that she would yield great influence over raising his kids. What kind of mother would she be? What would she teach the kids? What kind of values would she instill? What kind of behavior would she model?

The other thought that was high on Dan's list was how she handled money. Did she use money responsibly? Did she spend more than she had? If so, that was a big turn off to him and he felt he needed to move on.

Dating is the time to get to know someone, his or her habits, strengths and weaknesses, and evaluate the relationship for marriage. Remember that Eliezer observed and evaluated as Rebekah brought water to his camels. You, too, need to consider many things as you think about the future of your relationship. And of course, all this thinking is bathed in the prayer that we spoke about in the last chapter.

Ask yourself the hard questions.

Will this individual make a good husband or wife? Is she supportive? How does he treat his parents and other individuals? Will she be a good example for godly living to children? Will he show kids how to follow the Lord?

What might marriage to this person look like? Can you already see that it will be difficult? Does he make good decisions? Can you work out differences? How does she handle conflict?

Are your hearts being drawn together? Are you attracted to him or her? And incidentally, let me address this common concern. As you get to know an individual, you may find them more and more attractive. But you also don't need to worry that God is going to give you someone to whom you are not attracted.

Now, let's stop right now before we get carried away in evaluating and say that no one is perfect. You will not find that perfect mate nor that perfect relationship. As sinful human beings that is simply not possible. We have weaknesses, idiosyncrasies and we all make mistakes.

However, if you are really struggling in the dating phase with getting along with each other, putting a ring on his or her finger isn't going to magically make it better. If you are seeing red flags that tell you this is a no-go, you need to listen to the Spirit of God as He whispers in your ear. If you are ready, be bold enough to ask God to make you uncomfortable with the relationship if it isn't right. Ask Him to point out any areas of concern.

Maybe the person you are dating has things in the past that you are not exactly excited about. The key is to look at who that person is now. Is he or she the same person or now a different person? Maybe those things you don't like were actions taken before this individual knew the Lord. Just as he or she is forgiven in Christ, you need to forgive and move forward.

There is no rush. Take the time to evaluate.

If you have prayed, considered, thought through and in some cases, wrestled with the future of your relationship . . . if you have determined that this isn't the person that God has for you, then you must be willing to walk away. If at your core you know there is no future, you need to muster the strength to bring a conclusion to your relationship.

This can be so difficult, and if this is you, I can feel your internal struggle, disappointment and sadness. But better to end the relationship now than to drag it out and waste more time for both of you . . . or worse yet, to marry the person and wish later you could walk away.

Several years ago, Dan and I were building our dream house. We had sold our house, moved our family into my mom's home and started the process of designing and making all the fun selections that go with building your own house. We were one week away from breaking ground when my husband received news that his job security was . . . well, not secure. The company had been bought and was undergoing changes. His job in particular was at risk and all of the sudden we were facing the possibility of my husband losing his job when we were about to take on a giant financial responsibility.

Knowing my builder (who was a friend) started his day at the crack of dawn, I texted him very early the next morning. And at 6:30 a.m., he called me back and I explained our situation. He couldn't have been more gracious about delaying the project. But that didn't help my heartache and sadness.

I was concerned for my husband, for what he was going through, what job loss could mean for our family but also sad at the fact that we couldn't build the new house. We don't take financial risks or gambles. We purposely didn't even begin building until we sold the last house because we knew that we didn't want the potential stress of two mortgages. So obviously, building was off until one of two things happened: his job security was regained or he found a new job, which would require knowledge of his salary so that we could be sure of affording the project.

To tell you I was disappointed about not building the house I had worked so hard on is an understatement. I felt as if my hopes were crushed. I could not even drive by our new street. I purposely drove a different route when driving my kids to school because seeing the street where our house was supposed to be built was just too sad.

It took about three weeks before I could drive by without tearing up. But finally, I arrived at the place where I could say, "Lord, if that is not your will for us . . . so be it." So be it. I could finally say I wanted His will more than mine and that if I never built our house, it would be okay with me.

Sometimes through our evaluation, we may realize that even though we want something so terribly bad, it may not be right or it may not be the right time. This comes full circle to what we spoke about in the last chapter. If you want to know the secret to God's plan for finding true love, it is this: submission and surrender. It is yielding to the will of God, putting His desires above your own. It is not always easy, in fact it can be downright crushing. But the one glorious thing I can tell you is that it will always be for your good. He loves you. He knows you. He will do right by you over and over again.

My dear friend, yield and surrender all of your relationships to the loving care and authority of the Father. You will never be sorry. Incidentally, about six months later we did go on to build the house. The time of waiting actually allowed me to save up more money so that we could do granite countertops and install upgraded light fixtures—hidden blessings I would have never guessed possible if not for yielding and waiting.

Let's take a look at what happens next in our love story of Isaac and Rebekah. Remember that Rebekah took Abraham's servant back to her family's home. They sat down together and Eliezer shared his story. Upon hearing the detailed account, Rebekah's family agreed that this was the Lord's will. The next step was to return home to Abraham and Isaac.

> When they got up the next morning, he said, "Send me on my way to my master."

> But her brother and her mother replied, "Let the young woman remain with us ten days or so; then you may go."

> But he said to them, "Do not detain me, now that the Lord has granted success to my journey. Send me on my way so I may go to my master."

> Then they said, "Let's call the young woman and ask her about it." So they called Rebekah and asked her, "Will you go with this man?"

"I will go," she said. (Genesis 24:54b-58)

Here we see Rebekah's consent to be married to Isaac. I am sure Rebekah had been thinking and processing all the things that had happened, mulling them over, evaluating the situation. When it came to a decision, it was easy and it was clear.

The idea of marriage to both you and the one you are marrying should be exciting and entered into with great joy. There is no pressure, no stress, only excitement about the future.

> So they sent their sister Rebekah on her way, along with her nurse and Abraham's servant and his men. And they blessed Rebekah and said to her,
>
>> "Our sister, may you increase
>> to thousands upon thousands;
>> may your offspring possess
>> the cities of their enemies."
>
> Then Rebekah and her attendants got ready and mounted the camels and went back with the man. So the servant took Rebekah and left. (Genesis 24:59-61)

If you have carefully evaluated, sought the Lord and sensed His leading to one another, then praise the Lord. I am so excited for you! You are starting your marriage off in the right place . . . at the well.

Chatter At The Well

How will I know I've met the right person?

Everyone has a unique story when it comes to how they knew they had met the one that God intended for them. I have already shared that after seeking the Lord's will above my own in regards to my relationship with Dan, I felt the Lord's blessing and pleasure. When considering marriage to Dan, I also felt such a strong peace about the decision. I knew that the Lord was leading us to start a life together.

I asked some dear friends this same question and wanted to share with you their answers:

From Adrienne: In every previous relationship or instance of being interested in someone, I had always struggled with a lot of worry and anxiety that I would not follow God's leading, and that I'd be deceived into following my own heart and make a mistake by dating the person, or even by allowing my heart to like him. With Brian, I prayed as I had in the past, "Lord, please stop this if it isn't from you. Please guard my heart . . . ." This time, I felt God leading me to stop praying against it and begin praying for it.

From Missy: I remember praying from the first time Joe and I started dating that if God didn't want us together that things wouldn't work out and we would break up. Ultimately, I wanted what God wanted because I knew that *He knew* what was best.

From Tara: I knew I would not marry Jon until I was completely confident the Lord was leading me in this way. For me, it was more of struggle to come to this conclusion than Jon (who knew early on). But finally, I just knew. From that point on, I have never once doubted.

From Dan: When Kristen and I were dating, it was obvious that she did more than simply tolerate or accept my faith. She embraced it because it was hers as well. As I prayed about direction for our relationship, I talked with the people closest to me who adored Kristen and agreed about our compatibility. Kristen and I prayed a lot about it and we felt the Lord was leading us together. But it wasn't until I got that bonus check for the ring that I felt 100 percent sure. I was amazed at God's tangible leading and blessing.

From Hope: I knew right away. After previous relationships with unbelievers, Derek really stood out. We spent our first date talking about the Lord and I knew right then and there this was the guy the Lord had for me. I didn't have to push this relationship or try super hard to make it work. It just did. My dad had many "garage talks" with me about previous relationships to encourage finding the right man. When I met Derek, our "garage talks" came to an end.

From Sandy: Steve and I had been dating for three years and after seeing his good character and consistency, I knew the Lord was leading us to one another. This assurance only grew during our time spent together. So when Steve was being deployed, it was an easy decision to move up the ceremony and continue to plan the big wedding for after his return.

From Jarred: I had known Jody since we were kids, so the Lord was working all the way back then. We dated in high school on and off, but eventually broke up after freshman year of college. We got back together a few years later, shortly before I moved across the country for a job. However, even living on the other side of the country, I could see that Jody was committed to me. And then one Sunday morning, she called to tell me that she was saved while attending Easter morning services. At that point it was evident that God was preparing her to be my wife. It would be two years later that we would marry.

From Jody: Jarred and I had been dating on and off since we first met in fifth grade at Bible school. Despite the challenges we faced and the time spent apart while living in different cities, it never really felt like Jarred and I were far from each other emotionally or geographically. He was a constant in my life regardless of the stage of our relationship. I knew he loved the Lord and my relationship with God deepened because of his example. I think all along

I knew there was no other boy for me than him. God kept Jarred as an ever present force in my life for so many years before we got married and for that I'm so thankful. I knew Jarred was the one God had planned specifically for me and now, I get to spend every day with my best friend!

From Clayton: I had plenty of time while in the Marine Corps to reflect on my perfect wife. I created a list of important ideas and qualities I desired. When I met Sharon, I began to see them in her. I wanted to date (well really, get engaged and marry) her but the timing wasn't right for God's plan. There were many things I needed to fulfill in myself in order for His plan to happen. After approximately six years and about three attempts at dating, it came together. Sharon had once told a friend if she dated me, we would end up married. But when she kissed me the first time (after those 72 months of patiently loving her as a friend) I was certain where we would end up.

From Sharon: I had great fear of "knowing" if I would choose the "right" husband. Every interaction, conversation or date with a man was a subversive search for red flags and what to do about any flags found. I was poised to bolt. Clayton and I were friends before we attempted dating.

When dating didn't go well, it took a while to rebuild the friendship. A few years passed, we were at a number of the same events . . . having fun, understanding and enjoying each other! It was a turning point. God was at work—softening my heart and also changing Clayton's approach. Things started getting GOOD in a way that didn't work before! With my fear at bay, I could really see and appreciate Clayton in ways I had never imagined. Fear couldn't compete with all the good and every blessing that God was allowing us to have! I knew I didn't want to miss this adventure.

A Dry Bucket

Chapter Ten

A.K.A "WHAT IF YOU FIND yourself dating a non-Christian?"

If you find yourself in the situation of dating an unbeliever, then you have a hard decision or a hard road ahead. There are a couple of things I would like you to consider.

First, does this person you are dating know the importance of your faith? Have you downplayed or hidden it? If you have, I can already tell you that this is not a healthy relationship.

Second, measure the spiritual fervor of your walk. Are you walking closely with the Lord or are you more temperate in your faith at the moment?

If you're not feeling very close to Him, I want you to think back to a time when you were. Maybe it was after a retreat or mission trip. Possibly you're thinking back to a time when His answer to your prayer was completely evident or even miraculous. Ask Him now to bring back those thoughts, feelings and memories. Take a moment to linger there.

As you think back to that time, that moment, can we say that you would have wanted God's best for everything in your life? Would you have been willing to sacrifice the *good* for His *best*? Would you have told yourself to hold out and wait for the match that God has planned? I am willing to bet that you were in a greater state of surrender back then.

We know that God will never go against His Word and His Word clearly lays out as we have already seen that Christians are to be yoked to other believers. If you have made a commitment and intend to live for God in what you say and do, then you need to realize the future reality of this relationship. God will not tell you to marry someone that is not equally yoked in faith. He will not give you the go ahead to unite with someone who is not following Him.

Third, I want you to carefully think about a future with this individual, keeping in mind that we all put on our best behavior in early dating. Think about the state of his or her heart toward God. What happens in five years and you are starting a family and he or she drops the bombshell that your kids will not be allowed to go to church or when your kids start to show interest in the things of God and your spouse begins to resent it?

I pray that would not be the case, but I know it's possible and have seen it happen. It would be far better to remain single than be married and miserable.

When you have followed the leading of the Lord in choosing a mate and found the right person, remember the beautiful response we witnessed in the account of Genesis 24: the overwhelming heart of worship toward God. Eliezer worshiped when Rebekah, after drawing water for the camels, told him whose family she was from.

Let's also remember another result of a divinely arranged marriage: the confirmation of others. We saw Laban and Bethuel confirming that this marriage was indeed the will of the Lord. And we saw Eliezer once again worshiping when they said this.

Are you in a position to worship God for the relationship before you? Do you feel His pleasure and His blessing? Are you receiving confirmation from those to whom you are closest? If not, perhaps you need to reevaluate the relationship. Oh, how I wish we could sit down together and you could tell me everything that is going on in your head and heart.

So much to consider.

Chip Ingram, a pastor and the founder of Living On The Edge ministries, tells a story of a little girl who went on vacation with her family to the New England seashore. The family rented a cottage and you could step out of the cottage door right onto the beach. There was also a pier with a fishing boat and a little old man who would sit on that pier each day. He was a grumpy old man, mean and weathered by a hard life.

The little girl was about five or six years old and each day, she would walk down the pier with her little pigtails bouncing along as she went. She would greet the old man as sweet little children do. She would give him shells that she had found. And after a couple of days doing this, the man's hardened heart softened toward the little girl. He shared a bit of fishing line and they would sit together and she would dangle her feet off the pier.

These two unconventional friends developed quite a bond. The old man realized that no one else cared about him in life except this little girl. As her week-long vacation was coming to an end, he noticed that as she would dangle her feet off the pier, she would clutch the plastic beads hanging around her neck.

Now in all his time at the pier, he had found a number of shells and pearls. So that last night, he stayed up late, drilling holes and stringing the pearls together into a beautiful necklace.

When it was time for the family to go and the car was all packed, the little girl ran down the pier to say goodbye. The little old man told her that he had a present for her and he asked her to take off her plastic beads. He then held up the shiny pearl necklace.

Well, she just ran back to the car quite upset that the man was trying to take her beads from her, not at all understanding the value of the necklace the old man was trying to give.[15]

My friend, there are times in our lives where we want to hold on so badly to what we know and what is comfortable . . . or should I say *who* we know and *who* is comfortable. An unbeliever with a born again child of God is a string of plastic beads. God has pearls waiting for you. Be willing to surrender to Him and for your own good and your own joy, yield to His direction for your life. He is good. He is loving. He is faithful. Choose to follow Him in your relationships and truly, in everything you do.

Part Five
Living at the Well

Beautiful Blessings

Chapter Eleven

ARE YOU READY TO WRAP up our love story? Let's read the final portion of Genesis 24.

Now Isaac had come from Beer Lahai Roi, for he was living in the Negev. He went out to the field one evening to meditate, and as he looked up, he saw camels approaching. Rebekah also looked up and saw Isaac. She got down from her camel and asked the servant, "Who is that man in the field coming to meet us?"

"He is my master," the servant answered. So she took her veil and covered herself.

Then the servant told Isaac all he had done. Isaac brought her into the tent of his mother Sarah, and he married Rebekah. So she became his wife, and he loved her; and Isaac was comforted after his mother's death. (Genesis 24:61-66)

Here Rebekah, Eliezer and the others traveled back to Abraham and his family. On a journey that could have taken over a month, can you imagine riding on the back of a camel? Yikes! At least Rebekah probably had plenty of opportunities to hear Eliezer's stories about Isaac, the man God had chosen for her to marry. Maybe Eliezer told her about Isaac's good character, his submission to Abraham at the altar, his trust in God, his peaceful nature and life of prayer and faith.[16]

There are two very important things I would like us to notice in this passage. First, we learn in verse 63, that Isaac was in the field meditating. Many believe that this would be indicative of praying. Have you ever spent some time alone, maybe outside, thinking and praying . . . letting something roll around in your head as you have a quiet conversation with the Lord? I like Isaac already.

The second thing to see is that Isaac had come up from Beer Lahai Roi. No, he wasn't drinking as the name may indicate. It is pronounced BEE ear lah HIGH roy[17] and was the name of . . . a well. How beautiful that the Lord brings us full circle and we find Isaac coming up from the well.

Remember when we were talking earlier about feeling forgotten? Take a look at this. The meaning of Beer Lahai Roi is "the God who sees." This well, Beer Lahai Roi, was named when Hagar was fleeing from Sarah. The angel of the Lord appeared to Hagar and it is at this place that she realizes that God sees *her* and He hears *her*. It is the moment when someone else's God became her very own. The moment she became acutely aware that she was cared for by the Most High.

You may be feeling lonely in your singleness. You may be feeling like you are on the outskirts and everyone else is finding love. But God sees you. He sees *you*. You are not forgotten. You are not alone. Go to Beer Lahai Roi. Go to that well, draw your water and rest in the fact that the Lord of the universe loves and sees you.

Now, I wonder what Isaac was pondering as he had departed from the well and was out in the field. Was he thinking about his future? Was he remembering back to the close call on the altar of sacrifice so many years ago? Did he wonder how Eliezer's search was going? We know that Sarah had died and he was still grieving the loss of his mother. Whatever his thoughts, we can see that Isaac is contemplative and knows personally the God of his father, Abraham.

As the story unfolds, Isaac looks up and sees the camels approaching. Finally after hearing about Isaac for the last month, Rebekah gets to see him.[18] She asks who it is in the field and upon learning that it is Isaac, she veils herself. This is a tradition of modesty before marriage and a stunning reminder of the importance of purity and modesty even in the engagement phase of a modern relationship.

Now, being a former wedding planner I find the last few verses of Genesis 24 to be completely lacking. I mean, where are the details? Who all was present at the wedding? Was there music?

We know that Isaac must have felt as confident as Rebekah when the old servant shared the details of his trip. And we have seen how Eliezer is wonderful at recounting details as he did at the table with Bethuel and Laban. I wish this guy would have written the account of the wedding!

Despite my desire for details, the important things are shared with us. The servant told Isaac all that happened. Isaac took Rebekah into his mother's tent and married her. She became his wife and . . . he loved her. Isn't that beautiful? I could ask for no greater detail than to know this. He loved her.

God's design for marriage is this: to love one another, to do life together and to mirror the relationship between Jesus and His church. A husband and wife are to be helpmates to one another and to serve together. If blessed with children, God's design is to raise up a family in the faith and to teach the children, together, about the Lord (See Deuteronomy 6:4-9).

I love what Peter Marshall, a Scottish-American preacher and Chaplain of the U.S. Senate, once said about the oneness of marriage:

> Marriage is not a federation of two sovereign states. It is a union—domestic, social, spiritual, physical. It is a fusion of two hearts—the union of two lives—the coming together of two tributaries, which, after being joined in marriage, will flow in the same channel in the same direction . . . carrying the same burdens of responsibility.[19]

When you have found the one that the Lord has given to you for this beautiful union, you should feel such love and such blessing from the Lord. When Dan and I were engaged, it was an unparalleled time of excitement. I could sense the Lord's pleasure. Even the wedding planning was filled with blessings delivered from the hand of God. He provided in so many ways through others with things like invitations and musicians gifted to us by dear friends. The search for my wedding dress even fell under God's blessing and provision. It remains one of my favorite stories from that time . . .

When I was a little girl, I saved my coins in one of those giant Coca-Cola bottles. Did you ever see one? I threw all my extra coins and sometimes even dollar bills in the enormous piggy bank. Over time, I decided (in a very early-teen kind of way) that I would use the money saved to buy one of two things: my wedding dress or a dog.

Opposite ends of the spectrum, I know. But a girl's gotta have a dream.

So over the years, the big bottle grew heavier and heavier. I kept rolling and even came up with a clever little way of not having to dump the entire contents when I wanted to know how much I'd saved or roll up the newly saved coins. I rigged a little bag under the lid so that when I threw coins in, they sat in the bag instead of falling all the way to the bottom where everything was neatly rolled. Yep, clever. (If only I could be that clever with kid-clutter!)

Then came 2002 when I met Dan and after nearly two years of dating, he proposed . . . another fun story for a different time. The wedding planning began. We decided our engagement would be six months and these were my pre-wedding planner days, so I was learning as I went.

For those of you who have had siblings or close friends marry, you may know how much wedding budgets can vary. I had a tight budget. It was definitely a decent amount of money, but by no means luxurious. I have worked on weddings with a budget seven times what I had to spend.

However, when you are inviting about 400 people, that money has to stretch! Before I lose you to the insanity of 400 people, you should know that my husband's local family is over 100 people (our most recent Thanksgiving dinner totaled 132!). We invited everyone, even the children because we really wanted a fun, family atmosphere.

You should also know that my husband is one of those people who makes friends everywhere he goes. Seriously, the joke is that he can walk into a gas station . . . although who does that nowadays . . . and come out knowing the name of the clerk and a good portion of the person's life story. It is one of those things that I find endearing about him except when I'm trying to leave somewhere and he is in "conversation mode."

But back to the Coca-Cola bank and the wedding. Obviously, I would be needing a wedding dress before needing a dog. I added up my total of coins and bills and I came up with $402. Not bad . . . unless you're trying to buy a wedding dress instead of a dog. I went to many bridal stores. I tried on a lot of dresses but found nothing in my price range, especially when you consider that you have to buy a veil and slip too. I shopped the sales, the discount racks . . . but nothing.

I kept praying about it, believing that God would help me find the right dress for the right price. And that was when I heard about the Making Memories Bridal Gown Sale through Brides Against Breast Cancer. They had gown sales all over the country and proceeds helped programs supporting cancer patients and their families. Gowns are donated by retailers, designers, manufacturers and brides.

It was there that I found my wedding dress. The gown was beautiful! Strapless, detailed bodice, poofy skirt and a perfect-length train. And guess what? My total for the wedding dress, slip and veil was $397. Only God could have worked that out so perfectly!

The Lord gave us so much favor through other people's kindness while we were planning the wedding. When I think back to the way He provided, I stand in awe. But even greater than the provision of my dress, was the man that God gave me. Someone I waited a long time for . . . who had a heart for Him, was kind and full of integrity. Someone who makes me laugh still to this day. And in a blink of an eye, 13 years of marriage have come and gone. God is good!

So what can we conclude in all this? Blessings follow the obedient heart. It shouldn't be surprising. We can see over and over in the Bible that God blesses obedience. When we are seeking Him, He gives us the desire of our hearts.

Now where would I be if I didn't tell you just a little more about Isaac and Rebekah's life together?

Keep Digging

Chapter Twelve

A S DAN AND I HAVE grown over the many years and I think about how the Lord has blessed me with such a godly man, I want to thank and praise Him even more. Marriage has a sweetness when you're doing life not only together, but also with God at the head.

We know this doesn't mean life will always be easy. It will have its share of ups and downs. Even for Isaac. We see in the next two chapters of Genesis that Abraham dies, that Isaac and Rebekah deal with 20 years of infertility[20] and finally when God does give them two sons (Jacob and Esau), the two boys live in strife for much of their lives. We also learn that Isaac's family lives through a famine and Esau marries women who were idolaters and the women brought such grief to Isaac and Rebekah. No, life wasn't perfect.

But there was good as well. Isaac was the only Patriarch who took just one wife. The Lord God renewed the covenant with Isaac that He had made through Abraham. We know the Lord appeared to Isaac as well.

During the famine, God directed Isaac on where to live. In Genesis 26:12, we learn that "Isaac planted crops in that land and the same year reaped a hundredfold, because the Lord blessed him." No, life may not have been the easiest and mistakes were made, but the Lord was with Isaac. And I have to say that there could be nothing greater than to know the Lord is with you and your spouse.

Do you want to know what we see Isaac doing in Genesis 26? He opens wells. When the Philistines were jealous of Isaac's wealth, they closed up the wells that were dug during the time of Abraham. But Isaac reopens them. I just love that!

At Beersheba where the Lord appeared to Isaac, he not only builds an altar, but his servants dig a well. And later in verse 32, the servants tell him that they struck water. What joy that must have brought!

Opening the old wells, digging new wells. Even in the midst of a crazy life, we need to be digging wells, drawing closer to that place of God's presence and blessing. Our whole lives should be lived at the well. Every joy, every concern taken to the One who gives life-giving water. Our sustenance, our support, even our witness before others should be one of trusting and relying on Him who bought our redemption with His blood and lives still today.

I have often wondered how people who don't know the Lord get through a crisis situation. There have been times in my life where I could do nothing but fall limp against the stones of the old well. I was too weak to leave, too distraught to lift my head and at the well was my only source of hope. The Lord was faithful. He offered me everything that was needed.

When you are married, there will be challenges in your life. No one escapes this world without trials and tribulations. But a life lived at the well is the only true place of refreshment and respite.

Remember the conversation between Jesus and the woman at the well in John 4?

> Jesus answered her, "If you knew the gift of God and who it is that asks you for a drink, you would have asked him and he would have given you living water . . . .

> Everyone who drinks this [ordinary well] water will be thirsty again, but whoever drinks the water I give them will never thirst. Indeed, the water I give them will become in them a spring of water welling up to eternal life. (John 4:10, 13-14)

Stay at the well your whole life. Live there. Marry there. Raise babies there. Dig deep. Splash water on your face in the trying times and dance and play in the water in the good times. A life at the well is a life well lived.

So, what do you think of our Isaac and Rebekah? Have they inspired you to be found at the well in the midst of your love story? As you think on that, let's remember all the things we have talked about:

- Going to the Well—Before you are ready to meet the individual God has for you to marry, you must first be found in Jesus Christ.

- Growing at the Well—Deepen your relationship with the Lord and discover where He wants you to grow as an individual during this time of singleness.

- Waiting at the Well—Trust God to bring you the right person at the right time. Think about the characteristics that you value most in a marriage partner. Wait upon the Lord.

- Meeting at the Well—When you meet an individual, be in prayer, guard your heart, submit to God and seek the counsel of others. Take the time to properly evaluate your relationship for marriage.

- And finally, Living at the Well—As you and your spouse do life together, always be found at the well. As a couple, grow closer to the Lord and dig new wells.

If you have chosen to do these things, there will come a day when you stand at that altar and before you, will stand the most amazing individual. One who has been found at the well and chosen by the hand of God. The God who has seen you both has brought you together and you will stand in complete joy, knowing you have witnessed the pleasure of the Lord Most High.

A Letter to My Readers

D EAR FRIEND,

I hope you have seen that there is beauty in a relationship arranged by the Lord. It takes two people, two hearts who have sought the Lord, waited on Him and met each other at the well. Will this be you? Will you trust this area of your life completely to Him?

I can tell you that He is faithful. He is good. And He does not forget.

He is the source of life-giving water that will never disappoint.

The most important relationship you will have outside of your relationship with Christ is the relationship you have with your spouse. Be willing to wait on Him to bring you the one He is preparing for you even as you are being prepared for him or her.

I want to leave you with this verse:

"May the God of **hope** fill you with all joy and peace as you ***trust*** in him, so that you may overflow with hope by the power of the Holy Spirit." Romans 15:13 [emphasis mine]

How I would love to know if you have decided to wait at the well. Would you reach out and tell me? I believe someday you will have a beautiful love story written solely by the One who is the best storyteller of all time.

From one well-digger to another, blessings!

Kristen

Acknowledgements

MANY THANKS TO MY WONDERFUL husband and kids who have been excited for me to work on this project. I know the laundry has piled up and the refrigerator was emptier than usual, but your support has meant everything! Kids, when you're older, I pray that God speaks to you through these words and the beautiful story of Isaac and Rebekah.

Thank you to my amazing mom who gives endless support, encouragement and a fine eye for editing. You have always inspired my love of writing!

Thank you to my dear friend, Tara, who is the best of editors. I appreciate the hours you spent pouring over this book and hashing out the nitty gritty. This book is better because of you!

Thank you to my accountability partner, Jennifer Hayes Yates. It has been so fun to be on this journey with you. Thank you for all your prayers and encouragement.

Thanks to my friends and family who shared their stories with me, gave much feedback and prayed for me during this process.

Thank you to Phil and Erin of Design by Insight for creating a beautiful cover and to Kathrin Pienaar for use of her gorgeous photography.

Many thanks to Jen Henderson of Wild Words Formatting. Your knowledge and eagerness to help others is such a blessing to all authors.

Thank you, Janet Jacques, for your wonderful artwork found in the section divisions of the book.

And special thanks to Chandler Bolt, Sean Sumner and all those in the Self-Publishing School community. Your insight, advice and support has been invaluable.